QUAIL DISEASES

Identification And Management of Stress,
Vices, And Diseases In Quails

Contents

A quail bird is regarded to be in a state of good health when all of its body organs and systems are normal and perfectly functioning. Any alteration in the state of its body, or any of its body organs, which interferes with proper performance of its function(s) is what is regarded as **a disease**.

Since quails are flock animals, they have the potential to fast-spread any contaminated disease among themselves. This may negatively affect most quail farmers whose dream is to raise healthy and disease free flock. The benefits of raising healthy quails can never be over emphasized.

Below are some of the **benefits of raising healthy quails**:

- Production of high quality eggs and meat. I am sure you may not like seeing your quails lay eggs which have an attachment of parasitic larvae. You want to see them to laying clean and fresh eggs. Equally, you want them to give you quality meat.

- Healthy quails have inability to spread any contagious diseases among themselves, and to human beings.

- Healthy quails are vibrant, mature fast and have a longer lifespan. They are generally associated with high productivity.

- Healthy quails are cost effective to raise. You will have minimal bills related to their treatments/medications.

- Unlike sick quails, healthy quails have a higher market value. They fetch higher prices.

Without any experience, training, and proper equipments, an average quail keeper may be faced with difficulties in correctly diagnosing quail diseases and offering correct remedies. Therefore, in the next chapter, let's take a look at some of the observable physical (outward) signs exhibited by sick quails.

Signs of a sick quail

How can you tell that a quail bird is sick? A sick quail may exhibit several signs. You should therefore, be able to utilize the exhibited signs to roughly tell any of the diseases the affected bird could be suffering from.

Significantly, once you've clearly noted any of the signs that a quail bird might be unwell, you should immediately isolate it from the rest of the flock and speedily seek for the services of a trained and experienced veterinary professional for appropriate interventions.

Note: Always stay away from trying to offer prescriptions or treatments to quail diseases you aren't sure about. It might turn costly and possibly, lead to the death of the affected bird!

Below are some of the observable signs exhibited by sick quails.

Numb, un-alert, and unresponsive

Sick quails usually appear numb and un-alert.

They are generally unresponsive to any form of touch and will be seen lying down most of the time. But if standing, they will tend to exhibit an abnormal posture.

Reduced productivity

If there is a sudden drop in the number of eggs laid by the hens, that could be a strong sign of disease infection within the flock.

Very high or very low body temperatures

You should occasionally check the body temperatures of the quails to establish if any could be experiencing very high or very low body temperatures.

Such high or low body temperatures could be signs of disease infection.

Lack of appetite

Sick quails often lack normal appetite and resort to eating lesser quantities of feeds. At the end of the day, just by checking at the quantity of feeds left at the feeders, you can tell whether there is a sudden drop in rate of feeding of the birds or not.

Any noted sudden drop in the amounts of feeds consumed by the birds could be a positive pointer to a disease infection within the flock.

Observable defects in defecations

When the defecation appears bloodstained, that's a strong sign of internal infection. If it has an accompaniment of worms, that's a sign of parasitic infection. If it's hard, or watery, those could be signs of dehydration, and diarrhea respectively.

Difficulty in breathing

Blocked mucus membranes, or any observable/hearable sound suggesting difficulty in breathing by any bird could be a sign of a respiratory disease infection. Possibly pneumonia.

Rough plumage/falling feathers

If the feathers are falling off, or appear rough in texture, be sure to check the affected bird closely for possible disease infection.

Lackluster behavior

Sick quails tend to appear gloomy, and are usually disinterested even when you give them feeds or water.

Note: In order to effectively contain any outbreak of quail diseases, you should readily seek for the timely services of properly trained and experienced poultry vets. They will always have an invaluable role to play in helping you raise a healthy flock.

Stress in quails (causes and control)

Stress is any condition imposed on the birds making them to be uncomfortable. Stress causes disturbance and prevents quails from eating well. subsequently, it prevents female quails from laying well.

Causes of stress in quails

- Sudden extreme temperatures. Very hot or very cold temperatures.
- Sudden change of routine i.e. sudden change in type of feeds, feed locations and locations of waterers.
- Sudden loud noises like thunderstorms, loud music, noisy automobiles and low flying aero planes.
- Insufficient or total lack of feeds and clean water for drinking.
- Presence of strangers, pests and predators within the cages/quails' houses.
- Introduction of new birds in an old flock may stress the birds (both the old and new birds will end up being stressed out).
- Improper handling quails i.e. during culling or during vaccinations.
- Overcrowding in the quails' house may force the birds to compete for space, feeds and water. Subsequently, they will always be stressed out.

Controlling stress in quails

- Change daily routines gradually.
- Effectively, control diseases and parasites affecting the birds.
- Insulate their house to guarantee uniform temperatures throughout the year.
- Shield the quails from sudden noise.
- Gradually, introduce new birds into the old flock.
- Minimize access to the quails' house by strangers.
- Keep the correct number of birds per housing unit; with provision of adequate balanced feeds and enough waterers.
- Handle the birds gently during culling or during vaccinations.

Vices in quails (causes and control)

Vices are bad habits that quails develop due to their environmental exposure. The two most common quail vices are egg eating and cannibalism..

Factors that expose quails to develop bad habits.

- Idleness. An idle quail can easily turn destructive.

- Presence of broken or soft shelled eggs within the sight of quails.

- Long delay in the collection of laid eggs may tempt hens to peck them.

- Lack of minerals such as calcium and phosphorus in feeds may force the birds to peck them elsewhere.

- Overcrowding in the quails' house may force hens to lay eggs on the floor; and get tempted to peck them afterwards.

- Still, overcrowding may encourage some quails to peck each other in trying to remove external pests from each other.

- Introduction of new birds with bad habits into an old flock with no bad habits may make the old flock with good habits to acquire the bad habits from the new birds.

- Mixing birds of different age groups may expose birds of younger age to bullying by birds of older age.

- Presence of bright light in the laying nests exposes the laid eggs to be pecked by hens.

- Hens with disorders. Once a hen lays an egg and thereafter, starts to move around even before its cloaca retracts. This might excite other birds to peck it.

Controlling vices in quails

- Keep the birds busy by supplying them with green vegetables hanged appropriately within their house.

- Keep the light around, or within the laying boxes at minimum so that the hens may not notice the laid eggs. And collect laid eggs frequently from the nests.

- Cull and debeak any noted cannibal within the flock.

- Cull hens which exhibits prolapsed. Those whose cloaca takes time to retract after laying eggs, to avoid tempting other birds to peck them.

- Provide the birds with well balanced and nutritious feeds, containing all the necessary minerals.

- Keep the birds according to their age groups. This is vital to help thwart any temptation for bullying by birds of older age.

- Keep the correct number of birds per housing unit; with adequate balanced feeds and waterers provided.

- Dust the birds regularly to shield them from infection by external parasites.

- Keep the correct number of birds per housing unit; with adequate balanced feeds and waterers.

Factors to look into when culling

Culling in quails can generally be defined as the identification and thereafter, isolation or removal of unproductive quails from the rest of the flock.

Below are some of the most common factors which may necessitate culling. They should help you know which quails to isolate from the rest of the flock.

- Old quails exhibiting low production levels, and birds with stunted growth (poor growth) are perfect candidates for culling.

- Birds exhibiting signs of disease infections, and birds already confirmed to be affected by chronic diseases and injuries that render them unproductive should be culled.

- Birds exhibiting vices such as cannibalism and egg eating. Also, quails with unpleasant personality (very aggressive or very noisy) should be separated from the rest of the flock.

- Hens that consume lots of feeds but are poor layers are usually uneconomical to keep. They should be isolated from the rest of the flock.

Predisposing factors to quail diseases

Predisposing factors to quail diseases are factors which exposes quails to contract diseases. They are factors making it possible for quails to get infected with various diseases.

Below are the six leading predisposing factors to quail diseases.

Age

Did you know older quails are usually susceptible to infection by certain poultry diseases due to their weakened body defense mechanisms? Equally, younger quails are prone to infection by certain diseases due to their not-fully developed body immune systems.

Physical body injuries

Any physical injury on any part of a quail's body may make it susceptible to bacterial infection. Such injuries may be caused by other quails, the quail's owner, or even by the affected quail.

Environment

Very cold or very chilly conditions may make it possible for quails to contract respiratory diseases like pneumonia.

Sex

Did you know that due to their delicate body anatomy, hens are prone to more disease infections as compared to roosters? Especially when laying eggs, they are more prone to get infected by diseases in a dirty environment.

Poor sanitation

Unhygienic housing conditions may spur outbreak of certain contagious diseases like Coccidiosis.

Mixing of other poultry breeds with quails

This too may easily facilitate the spread of contagious poultry diseases within your flock.

Effects of diseases in quails

The negative impacts of disease infection in quails can never be overemphasized. One of the differences between successful quail farmers and the unsuccessful ones is the level of care and disease management that these two groups of farmers accord the quails. While successful quail farmers would do everything to prevent and manage quail diseases, the unsuccessful ones see this as irrelevant and wastage of time and money.

Below are just but a few of the negative impacts of diseases in quails.

- Reduced productivity due to inactiveness of the affected birds.

- Reduced market value of the affected birds. In case you intended to sell them, they will fetch very low prices when compared to healthy quails of similar age and breed.

- High mortality rate. The affected birds may end up dying.

- In certain instances, there could be the disastrous cases of spread of fatal contagious diseases to the rest of the flock, or even to human beings.

- Costly expenses incurred by owners of the affected quails on their treatments or medications.

Major classifications of causes of quail diseases

et's look at the broader classifications of the major causes of quail diseases.

The major causes of quails' diseases are broadly classified into five groups.

Nutrition based

Occur as a result of excess, or lack of relevant nutrients in feeds i.e. lack of vitamin D3, Vitamin C, and phosphorus may make younger quails to be susceptible to attack by rickets.

Physical causes

Occur due to physical injuries to the bird in form of body cuts, sprains and broken body parts like legs.

Chemical causes

Occur due to excessive administration of drugs (over dose), or due to administration of a wrong drugs to an ailment.

Protozoan causes

Diseases affecting quails as a result of transmission by vectors like lice, mites and ticks.

Bacterial and viral causes

Affect quails as a result of transmission by bacteria and viruses.

The most common diseases affecting quails
(symptoms, causes, preventions and treatments)

B elow are the most common diseases affecting quails.

Coccidiosis

Coccidiosis is a parasitic infection which has a severe effect on the digestive tracts of quails. The infected birds would generally slow down and eventually stop feeding. The disease is characterized by general weight loss, loss of pigmentation, diarrhea and sometimes, deaths of the affected quails.

Prevention and treatment

Universally, Coccidiosis affects quails and other poultry birds out of poor management of farms i.e. failure to keep the poultry house clean and dry. Coccidiosis mainly thrive where there is a buildup of wet quail droppings and in moist areas around water points and feeders.

Ensure the house is kept dry and free of wet quail droppings. Construct areas where feeders and water points are located using wires. This will ensure no quail dropping will easily accumulate within the house.

Certain quail feeds are laced with coccidiostat to help prevent the infection by Coccidiosis. To the birds which are not yet infected with Coccidiosis, the consumption of coccidiostat in the feeds allows them limited infection with Coccidiosis and thereafter, they are able to develop immunity against the disease should it come knocking.

Worms (capillary worms/thread worms/crop worms)

Specifically, the most dangerous of the worms are those that infect the lining of the birds' crop(s). Capillary worms, which are scientifically known as *Capillaria spp.* falls in this category.

The infection caused by capillary worms can never be diagnosed by just looking at the bird physically. However, when the crop of the infected bird is removed (or when the crop of a bird which has died of the disease is removed), and opened up, worms which appear thread-like will the seen lining across the tissue fragments of the bird's crop.

The infected birds often eat a lot but always appear as if they are starving. And in the last stages of infection, the affected birds often experience difficulty in breathing. These are the two most common physical symptoms of a bird infected with capillary worms.

Prevention and treatment

Capillary worms usually thrive in wet droppings and on wet areas around feeders and water points. The best way to control infection and spread of capillary worms is by raising the birds on raised houses with floors fitted with wire mesh. Wires do not permit accumulation of quails' wet droppings and thus, this will prevent the birds from picking the disease from the cages and minimize its spread, if any.

An effective treatment for capillary worms is to use a relevant wormer (de-wormer). Consult any trained and experienced poultry vet within your area for recommendation on the most appropriate wormer (de-wormer), since the names of these drugs differ from one country to another.

Histomoniasis

This is one of the most lethal diseases affecting quails. Histomoniasis is also known as blackhead, and is a protozoan infection which attacks a number of poultry breeds. In fact, it is usually referred to as a disease of the larger fowl unit.

Histomoniasis infects the liver of quails and immediately, starts to produce necrotic lesions which eventually results into fatal liver damage of the infected birds. The infected birds often respond with restlessness, poor appetite, loss of feathers and sulfur-like-colored droppings.

Prevention and treatment

Usually, infected chickens are the carriers of this disease. As a precautionary measure, avoid mixing quails with other poultry breeds under the same housing. Equally, you should carefully, introduce new flock to an old flock, as the disease might be easily transmitted from a new flock to an old flock, and vice versa.

It is most recommended that you use relevant wormers (de-wormers), to help in elimination of cecal worms, which are the carriers of histomoniasis.

The most effective treatment for histomoniasis lies in its prevention, since no effective medication has been approved for its treatment. Infected quails may recover from the symptoms of the disease, but they will remain its carriers.

Rickets

Rickets affects quails as a result of a nutritional deficiency. It mostly affects young quails and is specifically as a result of lack of Calcium, Vitamin D3, and phosphorous in the feeds.

The affected birds usually exhibit physical inability to move around, or have bow-like legs as a result of weak bones, hence inability to support their own body weight. In extreme cases, the affected birds may register breathing problems or possibly, suffocation occasioned by immobile breathing muscles.

Prevention and treatments

To effectively manage the disease, you will need to change the feeds, or supplement the feeds with oyster shells, and equally, give the affected quail's water soluble vitamin D3. Equally, you can expose the quails to sunlight.

Liaise with your local poultry vet for recommendations of the most effective drugs for containing the disease.

Respiratory Diseases

There are quite a number of respiratory diseases that do affect quails. The affected quails often exhibit difficulty in breathing, sneezing, coughing and teary eyes.

The best approach to help correctly diagnose these respiratory diseases is through consultation of a veterinary professional trained and experienced in handling quail diseases. This is very vital given that a lethal respiratory disease like an avian flu usually has similar physical symptoms to other viral infections. Therefore, if in case you misdiagnose it, then you can end up losing your entire flock.

External Parasites

There a host of external parasites affecting quails. They include lice, mite, ticks and fleas. Of these external parasites, lice are the most common. Quails affected with lice often scratch and peck on themselves without ceasing. Equally, they get distracted from normal feeding and this usually makes them get stressed and subsequently lead to weight loss, and loss of egg production.

Quails affected with lice have ruffled and dry feathers. If uncontrolled, birds severely affected by lice may end up dying.

To help control lice and other external parasites, you should occasionally examine the quails for the presence of the parasites, and dust them with the correct pesticides. Equally, ensure that their house is clean and properly dusted/disinfected with appropriate pesticides

How to effectively deal with pests and diseases affecting quails

Did you know the cost for treating a sick quail may sometimes be twice the price of the affected bird? You should therefore, adopt effective disease prevention measures as a remedy for containing quail diseases.

Below are ways to help you manage a number of quail diseases. In some instances, these acts if timely performed, will help you contain spread of contagious diseases.

- The moment you chose to negligently raise your birds under unsanitary conditions, then you should be rest assured that even the best of quail drugs, when administered, will always be rendered ineffective. This can never be overemphasized!

- Ensure the quails' house is always clean and properly disinfected. Wet and uncollected quails' droppings around water points and feeding zones may expose the birds to contagious infections like Coccidiosis.

- Equally, effectively dust the birds with appropriate pesticides to help in keeping external parasites away.

- Their house should be properly constructed to effectively shield the birds from wind, hot sun, rodents like snakes, and other domestic animals like cats and dogs.

- Construct the house with cold insulators to keep the house warm during winter, and provide enough ventilation to cool down the house during hot summers. Equally, the house should have adequate exposure to light.

- Always feed your flock on quality and well balanced diet. Ensure you purchase their feeds, and other feed supplements which contain the right amounts of nutrients needed by the birds. If you do this right, you should expect quality eggs/meat from your flock, coupled with hardy birds, resistant to a number of infections.

- Give quails clean and fresh water for drinking, placed at strategic locations where they do not need any unnecessary strain to have access to it. It is advisable to give them water at room temperature: avoid very cold or hot waters. They tend to avoid drinking such waters.

- When some quails begin to physically appear weak or gloomy, isolate them from the rest of the flock, as fast as you can, and closely observe them for any possible illness.

- De-worm the birds regularly using recommended de-wormers. This will aid in preventing infestations by worms and other protozoan diseases like histomoniasis, commonly referred to as black head.

- Debeak noted cannibals with the flock to avoid inflicting wounds on other birds; which may subsequently make them susceptible to bacterial infections.

Parting shot

Let me make this parting shot short and to the point.

It's proverbially connoted that prevention is better than cure. Once quails are infected by any disease, there are only two possible outcomes: losing them to the disease, or incurring costly expenses on their treatments or medications.

Why would you choose to lose your quails to preventable quail diseases? To be successful in quail farming and realize meaningful gains, you must aim to raise healthy birds. As already highlighted, the benefits of raising healthy quails can never be overemphasized.

Disease-free and healthy quails are usually highly productive. It is rewarding to raise healthy quails, but unrewarding and hurting to raise disease infected, unproductive and unhealthy quails.

The End